EMPOWERING ME

Focused Practice

Reading • Language Arts • Math • Science
Social Studies • Recipes • Juneteenth

Created by

Drake Lawson

Fillip Mull

Solomon Mull

ISBN 979-8-9853160-8-7

Dear Parent(s),

Prepare to embark on an extraordinary journey of learning and discovery with this incredible book! Explore the exciting world of learning with captivating activities in Reading, Math, Science, and Social Studies. Plus, discover the joy of family bonding through engaging recipes and immersive Juneteenth activities. Whether your child needs a refresher or is eager to explore new concepts, our activities offer both independent and guided practice to cater to their unique learning style.

Brace yourselves for shared moments of discovery and bonding that will create lifelong memories. Moreover, our book is a celebration of Juneteenth, a momentous occasion in history. Vibrant coloring pages tell a powerful story that your child can bring to life while accompanying handwriting sheets encourage them to retell the tale in their own words.

If you're searching for captivating activities to review and expand your child's knowledge, this book is an absolute must-have. We've carefully crafted it to inspire, engage, and nurture curious minds. If you have any questions about the activities, please contact me at mmull@maminomull.com.

Respectfully,

Dr. M

Reading

Phonics Pick

Directions: Say each word. Color the word box with / ă/ black. Color the word box with /ĕ/ red. Color the word box with /ĭ/ pink. Color the word box with /ŏ/ gold. Color the word box with /ŭ/ blue.

1	cat	elf	wig	jot	bus
2	mop	bum	leg	pass	hip
3	sub	zit	dot	bed	yap
4	rim	hop	gad	nun	sell
5	hen	at	kid	toss	hut
6	alp	bet	mom	gig	cup
7	sum	jam	yell	pod	biz

Long Vowels

Phonics Pick

Directions: Say each word. Color the word box with /ā/ gray. Color the word box with /ē/ green. Color the word box with /ī/ white. Color the word box with /ō/ orange. Color the word box with /ū/ blue.

1	said	quote	meet	pen	sick
2	met	Hip	cute	lot	ran
3	fed	Table	geese	pie	lens
4	rim	Us	zone	bale	deal
5	jeep	Mitt	few	happy	rote
6	moo	Set	lake	pine	mute
7	bike	Doc	bump	tail	peep

Short & Long Vowels

Phonics Pick

Directions: Say each word. Color the word box with /ă/ black. Color the word with /ĕ/ red. Color the word box with /ĭ/ pink. Color the word box with /ŏ/ gold. Color the word box with /ŭ/ blue.
Say each word. Color the word box with /ā/ gray. Color the word box with /ē/ green. Color the word box with /ī/ white. Color the word box with /ō/ orange. Color the word box with /ū/ blue.

1	lame	light	mull	mint	nope
2	hum	apple	keep	join	kind
3	loft	net	lime	ram	peak
4	clip	cot	tame	feed	bun
5	geese	day	load	hug	chop
6	sap	zip	pom	me	mule

Blends

Phonics Pick

Definition: A phonic **blend** occurs when two or more consonants appear together, and you hear each sound that each consonant makes in a word. Examples of blends include bl, cl, dr, tr, gl, gr, pl, sm, sp, and st.

Directions: Say each word. Color the box that has a **blend** in the word brown.

1	slap	bum	or	treat	twist
2	grill	cone	red	gulp	brain
3	mop	guilt	milk	gate	cheat
4	drum	peep	ripe	long	spray
5	blend	crape	kit	cup	tomb
6	lamp	him	gold	end	zig
7	some	jar	left	road	trice

Phonics Pick

Definition: A **diagraph** is two letters that make one sound. Examples of diagraphs include ar, er, sh, kn, th, ch, and wh.

Directions: Color the box that has a **diagraph** in the word orange.

1	perk	boil	hark	chime	thug
2	load	bird	clue	phat	check
3	win	shaft	pop	wreck	sung
4	shut	quiz	king	crash	field
5	graph	eat	sit	comp	hill
6	scalp	team	less	wind	mute
7	wrench	zin	yell	put	arm

Blends & Diagraphs

Phonics Pick

Definitions: A phonic **blend** occurs when two or more consonants appear together, and you hear each sound that each consonant makes in a word. A **diagraph** is two letters that make one sound.

Directions: Say each word. Color the box that has a **blend** in the word green. Color the box that has a **diagraph** in the word yellow. Color the box that has a **blend** and **diagraph** in the word orange.

1	dark	blind	clumsy	ore	sheep
2	speak	path	form	slum	drip
3	slur	lime	check	shop	malt
4	slide	trap	crime	plea	slot
5	fork	treat	lack	bird	sharp
6	that	meow	perch	out	might

Blends & Diagraphs

Phonics Pick

Definitions: A phonic **blend** occurs when two or more consonants appear together, and you hear each sound that each consonant makes a word.
A **diagraph** is two letters that make one sound.

Directions: Say each word. Color the box that has a **blend** in the word green. Color the box that has a **diagraph** in the word yellow.
Color the box that has a **blend** and **diagraph** in the word orange.

1	shark	climb	dump	store	sleek
2	speaker	panther	torch	slumber	thicker
3	front	chirp	math	stomp	painter
4	coil	sleet	slacker	bride	sharper
5	sprang	meow	perch	gout	snicker
6	story	sharp	left	road	spice

Phonics Pick

Direction: Fill in the blanks with a consonant to create a word.

1	ma__	__ig	__et	__up	fo__
2	__ot	la__	pu__	gi__	ve__
3	__ix	__en	ba__	lo__	bu__
4	__un	__on	ki__	__at	__en
5	pe__	__ull	__om	__ast	li__
6	di__	be__	to__	__uzz	ra__
7	__ip	__eg	a__	lo__	u__

Phonics Pick

Direction: Fill in the blank(s) with a vowel or vowels to create a word.

/ā/   a, ai, ay, a_e   /ē/   e, ee, e_e, ea, _ey
/ī /   i, _igh, i_e, _ye, _ie,   /ō/   o, o_e, _oa_
/ū/   u, u_e, _ue, _ew

1	l_m_	d_ne	fr_it	m_pe	fe_l
2	p_ _k	p_g_	g_ _t	t_m_	ra_
3	m _de	at_	gr_ _n	c_p_	m_l_
4	sl_y	bl_nd	dr_ _m	m_ te	so_ p
5	_at	gl_ _	h_y	p_n_	ma_d
6	thr_ _t	b_	g_me	n_ _l	p_ _
7	sl_ _n	bl_ _	thr_ _	s_ ld	m_ n_

Language Arts

Nouns and Verbs #1

Definitions: A **noun** is a person, place thing, or idea.
A **verb** shows action.

Directions: Label each picture as a **Noun** or **Verb**. Write the word on the line for each picture.

_____   _____

_____

_____   _____

Nouns and Verbs #2

Definitions: A **noun** is a person, place thing, or idea.
A **verb** shows action.

Directions: Label each picture as a **Noun** or **Verb**. Write the word on the line for each picture.

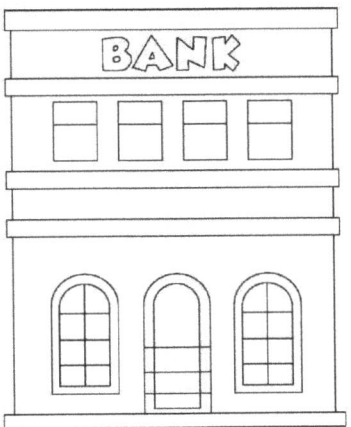

_____

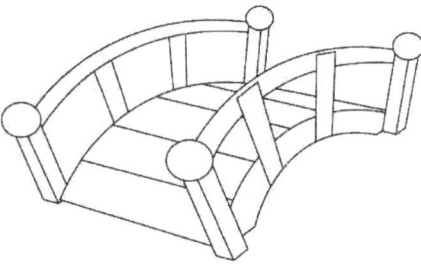

_____

_____

Nouns and Verbs #3

Definitions: A **noun** is a person, place thing, or idea.
A **verb** shows action.

Directions: Label each picture as a **Noun** or **Verb**. Write the word on the line for each picture.

_____

_____

_____

Nouns and Verbs #4

Definitions: A **noun** is a person, place thing, or idea.
A **verb** shows action.

Directions: Label each picture as a **Noun** or **Verb**. Write the word on the line for each picture.

Nouns and Verbs #5

Definitions: A **noun** is a person, place thing, or idea.
A **verb** shows action.

Directions: Label each picture as a **Noun** or **Verb**. Write the word on the line for each picture.

_____   _____

_____

_____   _____

Nouns and Verbs #6

Definitions: A **noun** is a person, place thing, or idea.
A **verb** shows action.

Directions: Label each picture as a **Noun** or **Verb**. Write the word on the line for each picture.

Nouns and Verbs #7

Definitions: A **noun** is a person, place thing, or idea.
A **verb** shows action.

Directions: Label each picture as a **Noun** or **Verb**. Write the word on the line for each picture.

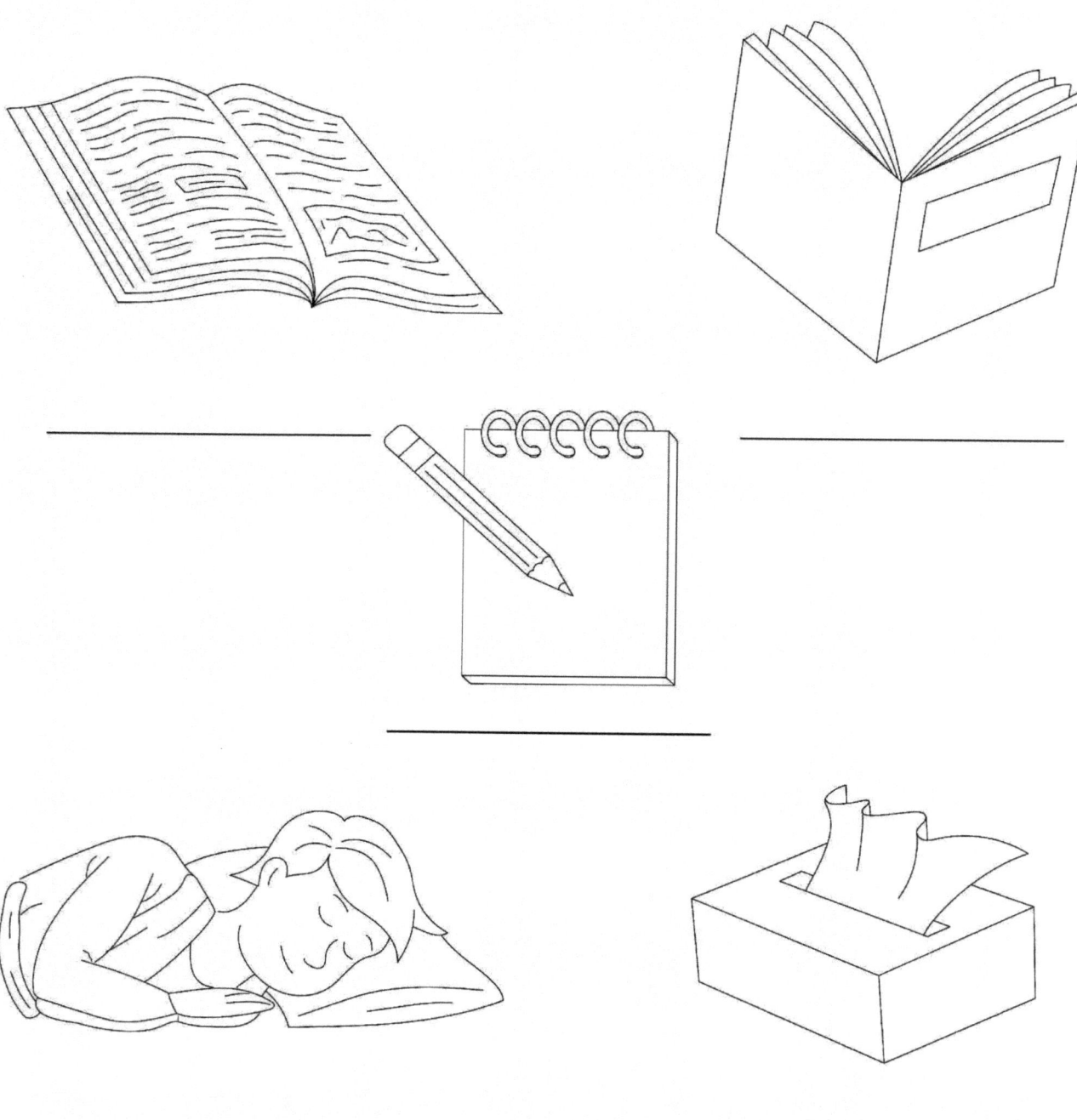

Nouns and Verbs #8

Definitions: A **noun** is a person, place thing, or idea.
A **verb** shows action.

Directions: Label each picture as a **Noun** or **Verb**. Write the word on the line for each picture.

Sentence or Fragment #1

Definitions: A **sentence** is a set of words that has a complete thought, contains a subject and predicate (main verb) and ends with a punctuation mark.
A **fragment** is a set of words that is missing either a subject or predicate (main verb) part.

Directions: Read each line. Write **S** for sentence or **F** for fragment.

Group of Words	Sentence (S) or Fragment (F)
the boy and girl are good.	
This is a great!	
by the table	
get it	
look down	
Mom and me	
you and I	
My friends	
he called my name.	

Sentence or Fragment #2

Definitions: A **sentence** is a set of words that has a complete thought, contains a subject and predicate (main verb) and ends with a punctuation mark.
A **fragment** is a set of words that is missing either a subject or predicate (main verb) part.

Directions: Read each line. Write **S** for sentence or **F** for fragment.

Group of Words	Sentence (S) or Fragment (F)
more than the other	
What did you say?	
I have	
Daddy and me	
Mommy and I	
The baby is crying.	
The tree is a big!	
Granny	
at school	

Sentence or Fragment #3

Definitions: A **sentence** is a set of words that has a complete thought, contains a subject and predicate (main verb) and ends with a punctuation mark. A **fragment** is a set of words that is missing either a subject or predicate (main verb) part.

Directions: Read each line. Write **S** for sentence or **F** for fragment. Turn the fragment into a sentence.

Group of Words	Sentence (S) or Fragment (F)	Fragment to a Sentence
stop talking		
on my desk		
I love you.		
He went to the movies.		
My birthday		
Which one did you like?		
don't you know		
Coco, my dog		

Math

Numbers 1 to 120

1											
					30						
						55					
											72
			88								
				101							
											120

Direction: Filling in the missing numbers.

Number Chart: Counting Backwards from 100 to 0

100									
50									
									21
									1

Direction: Filling in the missing numbers.

Matti has 3 balls. Alex gave her 5 balls. How many balls does Matti have in total?

Use the ten frame to solve the problem.

Use the number line to solve the problem.

Write your answer in a sentence.

_____
_____
_____
_____
_____

Who is the problem with?

What is the problem about?

What is the action?

How can I solve the problem (what operation, if applicable)?

Write a Number Sentence (e.g., $3 + 2 = 5$; $4 - 1 = 3$).

Kate had ten cookies. She gave six cookies to her brothers. Kate received some more cookies from her mother. She has twelve cookies left. How many cookies did her mom give her?

Use the ten frames to map out the problem.

Who is the problem about?

What is the problem about?

What is the action?

How can I solve the problem (what operation, if applicable)?

Write a Number Sentence (e.g., 3 + 2 = 5; 4 – 1 = 3).

Write your answer in a sentence.

Directions: Read the word problem. Fill in the information on the word problem mat. Filling in the information in each box will help you solve the problem. Record how you solve the problem. Write a number sentence. Write your answer in a sentence.

Gabbi read three pages in the book. Gisselle read four pages in the book. How many more pages do they need to read to complete the 10-page book?

Who is the problem about?

What is the problem about?

What is the action?

How can I solve the problem (what operation, if applicable)?

Use the ten frame to solve the problem.

Use the number line to solve the problem.

Write your answer in a sentence.

Write a Number Sentence (e.g., 3 + 2 = 5; 4 − 1 = 3).

Directions: Read the word problem. Fill in the information on the word problem mat. Filling in the information in each box will help you solve the problem. Record how you solve the problem. Write a number sentence. Write your answer in a sentence.

Kat has 8 dolls in her toy box. She received 3 dolls in the mail from her Granny. She brought 2 dolls with her birthday money. How many dolls does she have altogether?

Use the ten frames to map out the problem.

Who is the problem about?

What is the problem about?

What is the action?

How can I solve the problem (what operation, if applicable)?

Write a Number Sentence (e.g., 3 + 2 = 5; 4 − 1 = 3).

Write your answer in a sentence.

_____

_____

_____

_____

_____

Directions: Read the word problem. Fill in the information on the word problem mat. Filling in the information in each box will help you solve the problem. Record how you solve the problem. Write a number sentence. Write your answer in a sentence.

Counting by 2s with Odd Numbers

1						13			19
				29					
					51				
61									79
			87						
	103								119

Direction: Filling in the missing numbers.

Skip Counting by 2s, 5s, and 10s

Counting by 2s

2									20
				50					
									120

Counting by 5s

5									
									120

Counting by 10s

10											120

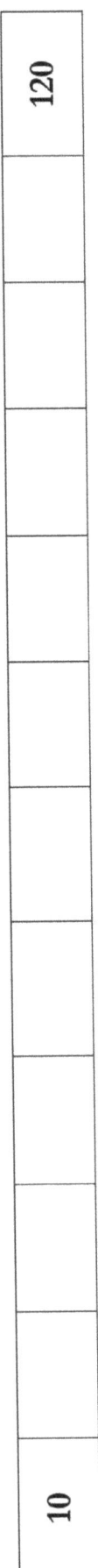

Direction: Filling in the missing numbers.

Number Chart: Counting Forward

201									
								250	
				285					
								320	

Direction: Filling in the missing numbers.

Lexi has a doll chest. She put 6 dolls in each row. The chest has 9 rows. How many dolls are in the chest?

Who is the problem with?	Draw an array to solve the problem.
What is the problem about?	
What is the action?	
How can I solve the problem (what operation, if applicable)?	

Write a Number Sentence (e.g., 3 + 2 = 5; 4 − 1 = 3).	Write your answer in a sentence.
	_____
	_____
	_____
	_____
	_____

Directions: Read the word problem. Fill in the information on the word problem mat. Filling in the information in each box will help you solve the problem. Record how you solve the problem. Write a number sentence. Write your answer in a sentence.

Pete went shopping at his favorite store. He has a shirt for $35. He has a pair of shorts for $49. He picks up a pair of socks for $12. His shoes cost $85. The taxes are $14.93. Pete gives the cashier $200. How much change will Pete receive from the cashier?

	Draw a picture to represent the problem.
Who is the problem about?	
What is the problem about?	
What is the action?	
How can I solve the problem (what operation, if applicable)?	

Write a Number Sentence (e.g., 3 + 2 = 5; 4 − 1 = 3).

Write your answer in a sentence.

_____

_____

_____

_____

_____

Directions: Read the word problem. Fill in the information on the word problem mat. Filling in the information in each box will help you solve the problem. Record how you solve the problem. Write a number sentence. Write your answer in a sentence.

Jay read 146 pages in the book. Tiff read 138 pages in the book. How many more pages do they need to read to complete the 300-page book?

	Use a Place Value Chart to solve the problem.
Who is the problem about? What is the problem about? What is the action? How can I solve the problem (what operation, if applicable)?	
Write a Number Sentence (e.g., 3 + 2 = 5; 4 − 1 = 3).	Write your answer in a sentence. _____ _____ _____ _____ _____

Directions: Read the word problem. Fill in the information on the word problem mat. Filling in the information in each box will help you solve the problem. Record how you solve the problem. Write a number sentence. Write your answer in a sentence.

Cassidy baked 12 dozen cookies on Friday and 6 dozen cupcakes on Saturday. Cassidy used 26 eggs. Each batch of cookie dough makes 36 cookies. Three eggs make one dozen cupcakes. How many eggs did Cassidy use for the cookies?

	Draw a picture to solve the problem.
Who is the problem with? What is the problem about? What is the action? How can I solve the problem (what operation, if applicable)?	
Write a Number Sentence (e.g., 3 + 2 = 5; 4 − 1 = 3).	Write your answer in a sentence. _____ _____ _____ _____ _____

Directions: Read the word problem. Fill in the information on the word problem mat. Filling in the information in each box will help you solve the problem. Record how you solve the problem. Write a number sentence. Write your answer in a sentence.

Science

Lava Lamp

Materials:
1 Empty bottle of water
Water
Vegetable Oil
Food Coloring
Alka Seltzer Tablet

Instructions:
1. Find or get an empty bottle of water.
2. Fill the bottle with an inch of water.
3. Then fill the bottle with 2 ½ inches of vegetable oil.
4. Then choose the color of food coloring.
5. Put 3-5 drops of your food coloring in the bottle.
6. Put the top back on the bottle.
7. Last drop half of an Alka Seltzer tablet into the bottle

Vocabulary Development:
1) Reaction: a process that involves rearrangement of the molecular or ionic structure of a substance, as opposed to a change in physical form or a nuclear reaction.

2) Compound: A chemical compound is a chemical substance composed of many identical molecules containing atoms from more than one chemical element held together by chemical bonds.

3) Density: Density is the substance's mass per unit of volume.

Questions:

Question 1: Do you think the water and the oil will mix?
Question 2: Why did the oil and water not mix?
Question 3: If any, what reaction do you think the water and oil will have when you drop the Alka Seltzer tablet in?

Plants

Materials:

Fresh Seeds (pinto)
Quality Soil
Quart Ziploc bags
Starter potting container

1 Mason Jar
1 Bottle of room-temperature water
Light
Coffee grains

Instructions:

1. Place 2 inches of potting soil into a small container or large tub, depending on how many seeds you want to grow. Lay seeds on top of the soil and cover with another ½ inch of moist potting soil. Moisten the soil with ¼ cup of water. Position the container in a sunny window.
2. Next, tear two pieces of paper towel. Fold the paper towel in half. Soak the paper with room temperature water. Place the 3 beans in the center of the fold of the paper towel. Position the paper towel with the bean inside the Quartz zip lock bag. Seal the bag. Tape the zip lock to a window with plenty of sunlight.
3. Place 2 inches of coffee grains into a mason jar. Lay seeds on top of the soil and cover with another ½ inch of moist potting soil. Moisten the coffee grains with ¼ cup of water. Position the mason jar in a sunny window.

Vocabulary Development:

1) A nutrient is a component in food that organisms use to survive and grow.

2) Photosynthesis is the process by which plants capture light energy and store it in sugars for later use.

3) Germination is the process of a plant emerging from a seed and beginning to grow.

4) Chlorophyll is the green substance in plants that makes it possible for them to make food from carbon dioxide and water.

Questions:

Question 1: What plant do you think will grow the fastest? Why?

Question 2: Which plant grew the most after 1 week? Why?

Question 3: Which plant received the most nutrients from its soil?

Question 4: What does a plant need to live?

Question 5: Does soil affect plant growth? Why does soil affect plant growth?

Question 6: What are the parts of the plant?

Living and Nonliving Things

Materials:

Crayons   Worksheet

Pencil   Dictionary

Vocabulary Development:

1) Living thing

2) Non-living thing

3) Classification

4) Alive

5) Dead

6) Life cycle

7) Needs

Questions:

Question 1: What plant do you think will grow the fastest? Why?

Question 2: Which plant grew the most after 1 week? Why?

Question 3: Which plant received the most nutrients from its soil?

Question 4: What does a plant need to live?

Question 5: Does soil affect plant growth? Why does soil affect plant growth?

Question 6: What are the parts of the plant?

Living and Non-living Things

Directions: Classify each item as a living or a non-living thing. Write each living thing under the column labeled Living Things. Write each non-living thing under the column labeled Non-living Things. Color all living things.

Living Things:

1. _____
2. _____
3. _____
4. _____
5. _____
6. _____
7. _____
8. _____
9. _____
10. _____

Non-living Things:

1. _____
2. _____
3. _____
4. _____
5. _____
6. _____
7. _____
8. _____
9. _____
10. _____

Sink and Float

Materials:

5-quart clear container
Pen
Banana
Empty water bottle
Full water bottle
Keys
Scissors
Ball
Apple

Strawberry
Crayons
Coin
Paper clip
Ball
Glue

Instructions:

1. Fill a 5-quart clear container or kitchen sink with water.
2. Evaluate the items above to find your answers to the questions.

Vocabulary Development:

1) Sink is a verb. In water, some objects sink to the bottom. Objects that sink have a higher density than water.
2) Float is a verb. In water, some objects stay or move above the surface. Objects that float have a lower density than water.
3) Density is a noun. It is how much mass there is in a particular space.

Questions:

Question 1: Which items will float? Why?

Question 2: Which items will sink? Why?

Sink and Float

Directions: Which items float? Which items sink? Color the items that float blue and the items that sink green.

OBJECT	SINK	FLOAT
PEN		
COTTON BALLS		
FRUITS		
EGG		
CAN		
FORK		
KEY		
FEATHER		

Social Studies

Community and Community Helpers

Materials:

Construction Paper
Scissors
Glue
Pencil
Markers
Chalk
Crayons

Instruction:

1. Identify a community helper or an occupation.
2. Create an object that is needed for the community helper or occupation. For example, a doctor needs a doctor's bag, a mail carrier needs a mailbag, or a barber needs clippers.

Vocabulary Development:

Define each word.

1) Community
2) Community helper

Questions:

Question 1: What resources are in your community?

Question 2: What resources are in the city?

Question 3: Who is your favorite a community helper?

Question 4: Why are community helpers important to you and your community?

Question 5: Can you name at least 7 community helpers? Who are the community helpers?

Enrichment Activity:

Directions: Sort the words in the table below into five categories: '-er,' '-or,' '-ist,' '-ian,' and 'other.' Write each word.

Word List:

teacher	painter	doctor	artist
singer	cosmetologist	librarian	professor
chef	scientist	baker	loan officer
barber	banker	firefighter	detective
surgeon	president	therapist	minister
cardiologist	designer	engineer	plumber
nurse	principal	cleaner	waiter
technician	biologist	cashier	meteorologist

-er	-or	-ist	-ian	other

Family Celebration

Materials:

Construction Paper
Scissors
Glue
Pencil
Markers

Chalk
Crayons
Pictures
Page Protector

Project:

1. Scrapbook
   A. Create a binder that has a Preface (explaining the importance of the book), a table of contents, summary/synopsis, and an Appendix (add additional information).
   B. Add pictures from a family trip, recipes, family heirlooms, etc.
   C. Have fun creating your book.

2. Interview the oldest member of the family or a grandparent.
   A. Interview Questions
      1. Where did you grow up? How long did you live in the area?
      2. Where did your parents originate from? How did your parents get to the area you grew up in?
      3. What was your parents' occupation? Where did they work?
      4. How was your life growing up? How many siblings do you have?
      5. Did you have any special interests when you were growing up?
      6. What is your level of education? What was your favorite subject?
      7. Did your parents talk about any of your ancestors when you were growing up?
      8. Did you have grandparents growing up? How often did you visit your grandparents? How would you describe your grandparents?
      9. Is there anything you would change about your childhood, adulthood, or parenthood? If so, what would you change?
      10. Did you work? Where did you work? How long did you work for the employer? What was your occupation?
      11. What did you like to eat growing up? Did you eat fast food, or was your food prepared at home? Did you learn to cook? What is your favorite dish to cook?

3. Family Tree
   A) Gather information about your family starting with a parent.
   B) Draft a family tree outline.
   C) Add information to a leaf (A box or rectangle represents a family member. Each family member will be connected by lines to represent relationships. Each shape is a leaf on the tree.).

Learning about your family gives you a connection to your heritage. It can help you trace your genetics. It is a good way to learn about your family history in relation to historical events.

Vocabulary Development:
Define each word.
1) Heritage
2) Celebration
3) Genetics
4) Family
5) Traditions

Questions:
Question 1: What is your family favorite celebration?

Question 2: What tradition does your family have for Easter, Thanksgiving, or Christmas?

Question 3: What is your favorite holiday?

Question 4: What is your family heritage?

Question 5: What is your cultural celebration? How do you celebrate? What does the celebration include?

Innovators

Directions: Print the name of the person on the first line underneath the picture. Write their invention underneath their name on the second line. Use the names in the box.

Sarah Boone   Garret Morgan
Octavius Catto   Benjamin Bannker
Marie Brown   Rebecca Crumpler
Fredrick Mckinley Jones

Name: _____
Invention:_____

Name: _____
Invention: _____

Name: _____
Invention: _____

Name: _____
Invention:_____

Name: _____
Invention: _____

Name: _____
Invention: _____

Name: _____
Invention: _____

Wall Street Enrichment Activity

Materials:

Construction Paper
Scissors
Glue
Pencil
Markers

Chalk
Crayons
Pictures
Page Protector

Project Directions:

1. Identify resources in your local community that are important to the community.
2. Collect items in your community from places like banks, malls, and grocery stores by taking a picture, and collecting brochures, advertisement circulars, coupons, receipts, etc.
3. Ask them to take a picture or put together a binder of things collected.
4. Place each item in a binder and label the items.
5. Name the city and identify the creation date.
6. Plan where people live, work, play, learn, shop, read, do art, grow food, and visit nature like parks, zoos, gardens, etc. This includes houses, jobs, parks, sporting events, schools, colleges (if applicable), malls, libraries, museums, restaurants, hospitals, churches, tourist attractions, new businesses, etc.
7. Balance various neighborhoods (housing), jobs, schools, traffic, and the environment. Make plans for newcomers (when new people move into a community or are expected to). Before making plans for a community, planners need to know many important things.
8. Create streets, highways, water, sewers, etc. When you create those items think about how many people use the streets near the school, library museum, and park.
9. Do not forget about the city government (mayor, city council, and law enforcement.)

Project Collection:

A. Create a binder that has a Preface (explaining the importance of the book), a table of content, summary/synopsis, and an Appendix (add additional information).
B. Add pictures from the community that you want to use.
C. Have fun creating your book.

This project is centered around self-sustaining a community by focusing on its strength. Learning about economics is vital. Creating a city helps you learn economic hope and success. To thrive as a person, community, or city, everyone must learn to support one another as well as have access to resources, savings, housing, jobs, education, and health care. This project could be the start of your journey as an entrepreneur.

Vocabulary Development:

Define each word.
1) Savings
2) Resources
3) Housing
4) Neighborhood
5) Health care
3) Entrepreneurship
4) Economics
6) City
7) Community

Questions:

(The questions below will help you with creating your community.)

Question 1: Where can some people live? What types of shelters: apartments, houses, condominiums, etc.?

Question 2: Where do some people work? What jobs are needed to make a community or city thrive? Where do students go to school…elementary, middle, high school, college, or vocational training?

Question 3: What transportation (car, bus, train, or bike) is needed in the community or city?

Question 4: What can people do for recreational fun? Will the recreational activities be outside or inside? Will the recreational activities be at parks, stadiums, museums, etc.?

Question 5: Where will people go for food? Will the community or city use a garden? Will the city rely on restaurants?

Question 6: How can a business, community, or city be prepared for disasters like fires, floods, earthquakes, tornados, etc.?

Question 7: Should the community or city focus on drainage, garbage, sewage, or recycling?

Trivia Questions

1. Who was the first African American to earn a medical degree?
   a. Dr. Rebecca Crumpler
   b. Dr. Alfreda Webb
   c. Dr. James McCune Smith
   d. Dr. Daniel Hale

2. Who was the first African American ballet dancer?
   a. Misty Copeland
   b. Janet Collins
   c. Mlle de Lafontaine
   d. Lydia Abarca

3. In what city in Texas did the Black Soldiers hear about their freedom?
   a. Dallas
   b. Houston
   c. Galveston
   d. Prairie View

4. Who wrote "Lift Every Voice & Sing" aka the Negro National Anthem?
   a. Langston Hughes
   b. James Weldon Johnson
   c. Booker T Washington
   d. Maya Angelou

5. What was the second historically Black sorority and fraternity (Divine Nine)?
   a. Alpha Kappa Alpha and Alpha Phi Alpha
   b. Phi Beta Sigma and Zeta Phi Beta
   c. Delta Sigma Theta and Kappa Alpha Psi
   d. Delta Sigma Theta and Omega Psi Phi

6. What travel guide did African Americans use, with publishing between 1936-1966?
   a. The Travel Expo
   b. The Green Book
   c. The Blue Book
   d. The Colored Travelers Guide

7. What was the first Historically Black College/University (HBCU) in the United States to officially issue degrees to African Americans?
   a. Shaw University
   b. Lincoln University of Pennsylvania
   c. Cheyney University of Pennsylvania
   d. Howard University

8. Madame CJ Walker was the first African American female _____.
   a. Self-made millionaire
   b. Graduate from an integrated high school
   c. Self-made billionaire
   d. To own property in Ohio

9. Who was the first African American Senator in 1968? What state did he or she represent in Congress?
   a. Shirley Chisolm, New York
   b. Hattie McDaniel, California
   c. Hiram Rhodes Revels, Mississippi
   d. Thurgood Marshall, Maryland

10. What was the first Black Owned Record Label that operated, distributed, and marketed to African Americans?
   a. Black Swan Records
   b. Motown Records
   c. Sugar Hill Records
   d. Stax Records

11. What year was Black History Month recognized by a president?
   a. 1776
   b. 1986
   c. 1976
   d. 2006

12. Who was the first African American to seek the nomination for president of the United States?
   a. Barak Obama
   b. Jessie Jackson
   c. Colin Powell
   d. Shirley Chisholm

13. The Apollo Theater was opened in what city?
   a. Los Angeles, CA
   b. Harlem, NY
   c. Atlanta, GA
   d. Chicago, IL

14. What was Black History Month's original name?
   a. Negro History Week
   b. Negro History Month
   c. Black History
   d. Colored Month

15. What TV show is known for highlighting Historically Black Colleges/Universities, where the students attended Hillman University?
   a. A Different World
   b. Black-ish
   c. Fresh Prince
   d. The Cosby Show

16. Who invented the three-way traffic light?
    a. George Washington Carver
    b. Garrett Morgan
    c. George Monroe
    d. William Robinson

17. Why was Black History Month placed in February?
    a. It was the shortest month.
    b. It was close to the beginning of the new year.
    c. It was the same month as the birthdays of Abraham Lincoln and Fredrick Douglass.
    d. It was the same month as the March on Washington.

18. Alexa Irene Canady was the first _____.
    a. African American women's specialist
    b. African American woman cardiologist
    c. African American OB/GYN
    d. African American woman neurosurgeon

19. What was the location of the First Black Wall Street?
    a. Memphis, TN
    b. Houston, TX
    c. Chicago, IL
    d. Tulsa, Ok

20. How many estimated Union Troops arrived in Galveston Bay, Texas, on June 19, 1865?
    a. 1,000
    b. 2,000
    c. 12, 000
    d. 20,000

Bonus:
    Who was the first Black butler in the White House?
    a. Eugene Charles Allen
    b. Alonzo Fields
    c. Wilson Roosevelt Jerman
    d. James Hemings

Recipes

Buttermilk Waffles

Ingredients:
2 cups of flour
1 ¼ teaspoons of salt
4 teaspoons of baking powder
3 tablespoons of sugar
4 tablespoons of butter (not margarine)
2 large eggs
1 cup of buttermilk
½ cup of water
2 teaspoons of vanilla extract

Directions:
1. Combine the flour, salt, baking powder, and sugar in a mixing bowl.
2. Melt the butter in a measuring cup before you add it to the dry mix.
3. Add the eggs (warm temperature).
4. Add the buttermilk (use the same measuring cup as the butter).
5. Add the water (using the same measuring cup as the butter and buttermilk).
6. Add the vanilla extract.
7. Preheat the waffle iron.

This recipe will make four regular-sized waffles.

Homemade Syrups

Ingredients:
1 cup of water
¾ cup of brown sugar + 2 tablespoons
1 cup of white sugar + 2 tablespoons
¼ cup of buttermilk
½ cup of butter + 2 tablespoons

Directions:
- Maple Syrup
  1. Combine the water and 1 cup of sugar plus ¾ cup of brown sugar in a pot. Boil to a boil.
  2. Stir in the ½ cup of butter to water and sugar mix.

- Caramel Buttermilk Syrup
  1. Combine the buttermilk and tablespoons of sugar in another pot. Bring to a boil.
  2. Stir in the 2 tablespoons of butter to the buttermilk and sugar mix.
  3. Add ¼ of baking soda and 1 teaspoon of vanilla extract (it will bubble up).

- The Syrups
  1. Take 2 or 3 tablespoons of foam from the Caramel Buttermilk Syrup and add it to the Maple Syrup*. You can serve the remaining syrup as Caramel Buttermilk Syrup.

You can adjust the foam based on your taste.

Kid Friendly Macaroni and Cheese (4 serving sizes)

Noodle Water and Noodles:
3 cups of water
2 teaspoons of salt
1 tablespoon of vegetable oil
1 cup of elbow noodles

Seasonings:
¼ teaspoon of Cajun seasoning (seasoning salt if you do not have Cajun seasoning)
¼ teaspoon of garlic powder
½ teaspoon of black pepper
1 teaspoon of salt

Cheese Sauce:
½ cup of heavy whipping cream
½ cup of milk (2% or whole)
5 tablespoons of butter (not margarine)
½ cup of Gouda cheese
¼ cup of cheddar cheese
2 oz. of Velveeta cheese

Directions:
1. Combine the water, salt, and vegetable oil. Bring to a boil before adding the noodles. Boil for 14 minutes.
2. Keep ¼ cup of the noodle water.
3. Rinse the noodles once in a drainer.
4. Put the noodles back in the pot. Add the noodle water.
5. Add the butter (melted).
6. Add salt, garlic powder, Cajun seasoning, and black pepper.
7. Add the heavy whipping cream and milk.
8. Add the different cheeses.
9. Preheat the oven to 350°. Bake for 5 to 8 minutes to melt the cheese.

You can adjust the seasoning and cheese based on your taste.

Fried Chicken Chunks

Ingredients:
1 teaspoon of black pepper
½ teaspoon of garlic powder
½ teaspoon of onion powder
½ teaspoon seasoning salt
¼ teaspoon of salt
2 boneless chicken breasts
1 cup of flour
1 tablespoon of ranch seasoning powder
1 teaspoon of poultry seasoning
Great Value Vegetable Oil (This oil fries the chicken better than Wesson, Crisco, or other brands.)

Directions:

- Step 1
  Cut the chicken breast into 1 ½ inch pieces. Place the chicken in a medium bowl. Combine the black pepper, onion powder, garlic powder, salt, and seasoning salt. Toss the chicken and spice mixture until the chicken is coated. Place in a Ziploc bag and chill for 24 hours.

- Step 2
  Set the chicken out until the it becomes room temperature. Combine the flour, ranch seasoning powder, and poultry seasoning in a Ziploc bag. Heat the oil. Fry the chicken in batches for 7 to 10 minutes or until golden brown and done. Drain in a pan over a paper towel.

Kid Friendly Pizza

Ingredients:
Garlic Toast
Pepperoni
Cheese of choice
1 cup of Pizza Sauce or 1 can of Tomato Paste
1 tablespoon of sugar
¼ teaspoon of black pepper
¼ teaspoon of basil
¼ teaspoon of oregano
¼ teaspoon of parsley
⅛ teaspoon of Italian seasoning
⅛ teaspoon of salt

Directions:
1. Add the seasonings and sugar to the pizza sauce or tomato paste.
2. Spread the sauce on the garlic toast.
3. Add the cheese.
4. Add the pepperoni or other meat of your choice.
5. Bake for 8 to 10 minutes or until golden brown.

FYI do not use TOMATO SAUCE because the sauce is watery, and your toast will be soggy. I use both pizza sauce and tomato sauce.

You can adjust the seasoning based on your taste.

Friendly Cauliflower Pizza

Ingredients:
Cauliflower (whole)
1 to 1 ½ tablespoons of olive oil or 2 tablespoons of butter
Pepperoni or Italian Sausage or Ground Beef
Cheese (Mozzarella, Cheddar, Italian, etc.)
1 cup of pizza sauce or 1 can of tomato paste
1 tablespoon of sugar
¼ teaspoon of black pepper
¼ teaspoon of basil
¼ teaspoon of oregano
¼ teaspoon of parsley
⅛ teaspoon of Italian seasoning
⅛ teaspoon of salt

Cauliflower Directions:
1. Wash the cauliflower with water and vinegar.
2. Dry the cauliflower.
3. Cut the cauliflower into four pieces (1 inch thick).
4. Drizzle or brush olive oil or butter…top/bottom and sides.
5. Sprinkle salt, garlic salt, pepper, or seasoning of your choice on top and bottom.
6. Bake on each side for 10 minutes at 350°.

Pizza Sauce Directions:
1. Add the seasonings and sugar to the pizza sauce or tomato paste.
2. Spread the sauce on the cauliflower.
3. Add the cheese.
4. Add the pepperoni, cooked sausage, or ground beef.
5. Bake for 10 to 12 minutes or until golden brown.

FYI do not use TOMATO SAUCE because the sauce is watery, and your toast will be soggy. I use pizza sauce and tomato paste.
You can adjust the seasoning based on your taste.

Cookies and Cream Ice Cream

Ingredients:
1 cup of vanilla ice cream
8 Oreos

Materials:
Measuring Cup
Sandwich Ziploc Bags
Ice Cream Scooper or Big tablespoon
Teaspoon
Bowl

Directions:

- Step 1
  Put the Oreo cookies in a sandwich Ziploc bag. Put the Ziploc cookie bag into another sandwich bag. Crush the cookies with a canned good. Flip the bag to prevent the sandwich bags from having holes.

- Step 2
  Scoop the ice cream and place the ice cream into the bowl. Add the crushed Oreo cookies. Stir the ice cream and cookies.

You can add more Oreo cookies or ice cream per your taste.

Enjoy your treat!!!

Popcorn Balls

Ingredients:
2-3.0 oz bag of plain microwave popcorn
6 tablespoons of butter
1 ½ cup of mini marshmallows
½ cup of sugar
¾ cup of corn syrup
2 teaspoons of vanilla extract
2 tablespoons of water* (optional, add if it is too thick to pour)

Materials:

Measuring Cup   Cookie Sheet
Mixing Bowl   2 ½ quart pot
Wax Paper

Directions:

- Step 1: Sticky Mix
  Melt the butter. Melt the marshmallows. Stir the butter, sugar, corn syrup, vanilla extract, and marshmallows together. Bring to a boil for 3 to 4 minutes. Keep the mix warm.

- Step 2: Popcorn
  Pop the popcorn in the microwave. Keep the popcorn warm in the oven at 200°.

- Step 3: Making the Popcorn Ball
  Fold the warm popcorn into the warm sticky mix. Take the popcorn and form a ball. You can keep adding the popcorn based on the size of the ball you want.

- Step 4: Drying the Popcorn Ball
  Tear the wax paper. Place the wax paper on the cookie sheet. Sit the popcorn ball on the wax paper to set and dry. Then wrap in plastic wrap.

*__Do not__ use margarine because margarine has water. The water will make the popcorn soggy. *

You can add more popcorn or snacks per your taste.
Enjoy your treat!!!

Sweet and Salty Popcorn Balls

Ingredients:
2-3.0 oz bag of plain microwave popcorn
6 tablespoons of butter
1 ½ cup of mini marshmallows
½ cup of sugar
¾ cup of corn syrup
2 teaspoons of vanilla extract
2 tablespoons of water* (optional, add if it is too thick to pour)
¾ cup of pretzels (mini)
¾ cup of M&M's (mini)

Materials:

Measuring Cup	Wax Paper	2 ½ quart pot
Mixing Bowl	Cookie Sheet	

Directions:

- Step 1: Sticky Mix
  Melt the butter. Melt the marshmallows. Stir the butter, sugar, corn syrup, vanilla extract, and marshmallows together. Bring to a boil for 3 to 4 minutes. Keep the mix warm.

- Step 2: Popcorn
  Pop the popcorn in the microwave. Keep the popcorn warm in the oven at 200°.

- Step 3: Snack Mix
  Mix the snack of choice in a bowl.

- Step 4: The Mixture
  Mix the popcorn and snack mix.

- Step 5: Making the Popcorn Ball
  Fold the popcorn into the sticky mix. Take the popcorn and form a ball. Add in the snack mix. You can keep adding the popcorn and snack mix based on the size of the ball you want.

- Step 6: Drying the Popcorn Ball
  Tear the wax paper. Place the wax paper on the cookie sheet. Sit the popcorn ball on the wax paper to set and dry. Then wrap in plastic wrap.

***Do not** use margarine because margarine has water. The water will make the popcorn soggy.*

You can add more popcorn or snacks per your taste.

Enjoy your treat!!!

All Things Cheese Popcorn Treat

Ingredients:
2 -3.0 oz bag of plain or organic microwave popcorn
½ cup of Cheetos
½ cup of Doritos (get the Mini)
½ cup of Cheddar Chex Mix or Cheez IT Snack Mix
2 tablespoons of Popcorn Cheese Seasoning (Walmart)
5 tablespoons of butter

Materials:
Measuring Cup   Ziploc Sandwich Bags
2 Mixing Bowls

Directions:
- Step 1: Snack Mix
  Mix all cheese snacks of choice in a bowl. Break the Cheetos and Doritos into pieces.

- Step 2: Popcorn
  Pop the popcorn in the microwave. Keep the popcorn.

- Step 3: Cheese Seasoning
  Sprinkle the cheese mix over the popcorn. Toss the popcorn and cheese mix bowl. *You can sprinkle more based on your taste.*

- Step 4: Mixing the Bowls
  Mix the popcorn and snack mix. Take the popcorn and form a ball. Add in the snack mix. You can keep adding the popcorn and snack mix to the bag.

***Adding the butter is optional.** If you use butter, **do not** use margarine because margarine has water. The water will make the popcorn soggy. **I like my mix without butter**.*

You can add more popcorn or snacks per your taste.

Enjoy your treat!!!

All Things Chocolate Popcorn Treat

Ingredients:
2-3.0 oz bag of plain or organic microwave popcorn
2 tablespoons of butter
3 tablespoons of whole mix
1 ½ cup of chocolate chips
½ cup of chocolate chips cookie
½ cup of Oreos (mini)
½ cup of M&M's (plain)
½ cup of M&M's (peanuts)
1 to go pack of instant coffee (optional)

Materials:

Measuring cup	Ziploc Sandwich Bags
2 Mixing Bowls	Wax Paper
Cookie Sheet	
2 ½ quart pot	

Directions:

- Step 1: Snack Mix
  Mix the chocolate snacks of choice in a bowl. If you do not use the mini, you will have to break the cookies into half pieces. *You can mix other chocolates into your mix.*

- Step 2: Popcorn
  Pop the popcorn in the microwave. Keep the popcorn warm in oven at 200°.

- Step 3: Chocolate Melt (optional)
  Put the butter and milk in the pot. Pour in the chocolate and melt the chocolate chips. Use a fork to drizzle the chocolate over the popcorn. Let it dry on the wax paper on top of the cookie sheet.

- Step 4: The Mixture
  Mix the popcorn and snack mix. Add in the snack mix. You can keep adding the popcorn and snack mix to the bag.

- Step 5: Chocolate Taste (optional)
  Sprinkle coffee grains in the mix.

You can add more popcorn or chocolate snacks per your taste.

Enjoy your treat!!!

Old Fashion Popcorn

Ingredients:
½ cup of popcorn
1 tablespoon of butter
1 ½ tablespoons of vegetable oil
¼ teaspoon of salt

Materials:

Measuring cups
1 Mixing Bowl

2-quart set or Cast-Iron Skillet
Stove

Directions:

- Step 1: Preheat the pot or skillet.
  Turn the stove on to medium 6 to 8. If you are a beginner, a pot will be your best option. Keep the heat consistent.

- Step 2: The Oil Mix
  Add the oil. Add the butter. Pour in the popcorn. Sprinkle the salt. Cover the pot.

- Step 3: Resting
  It will take about 2 minutes to heat up. The popcorn's cook time is 5 minutes.

- Step 4: The Balancing Act
  When the popcorn starts popping, shake the covered pot and raise the lid about an inch to let the steam out (it pops better and faster). Keep the heat consistent. Shake the pot. Pour the popped popcorn into a bowl when the pot is half full. Shake the pot. Put the pot back on the stove. Repeat.

- Step 5: Popcorn Treats
  If you are making popcorn balls or treats, keep the popcorn warm on the stove. Mix your cheese mix, chocolate mix, hot mix, or your mix of choice. Then mix the popcorn and snack mix. Follow the directions on the previous page for Popcorn Balls, All Things Cheese, or All Things Chocolate.

***Do not** use margarine because margarine has water. The water will make the popcorn soggy.*

Coloring Pages

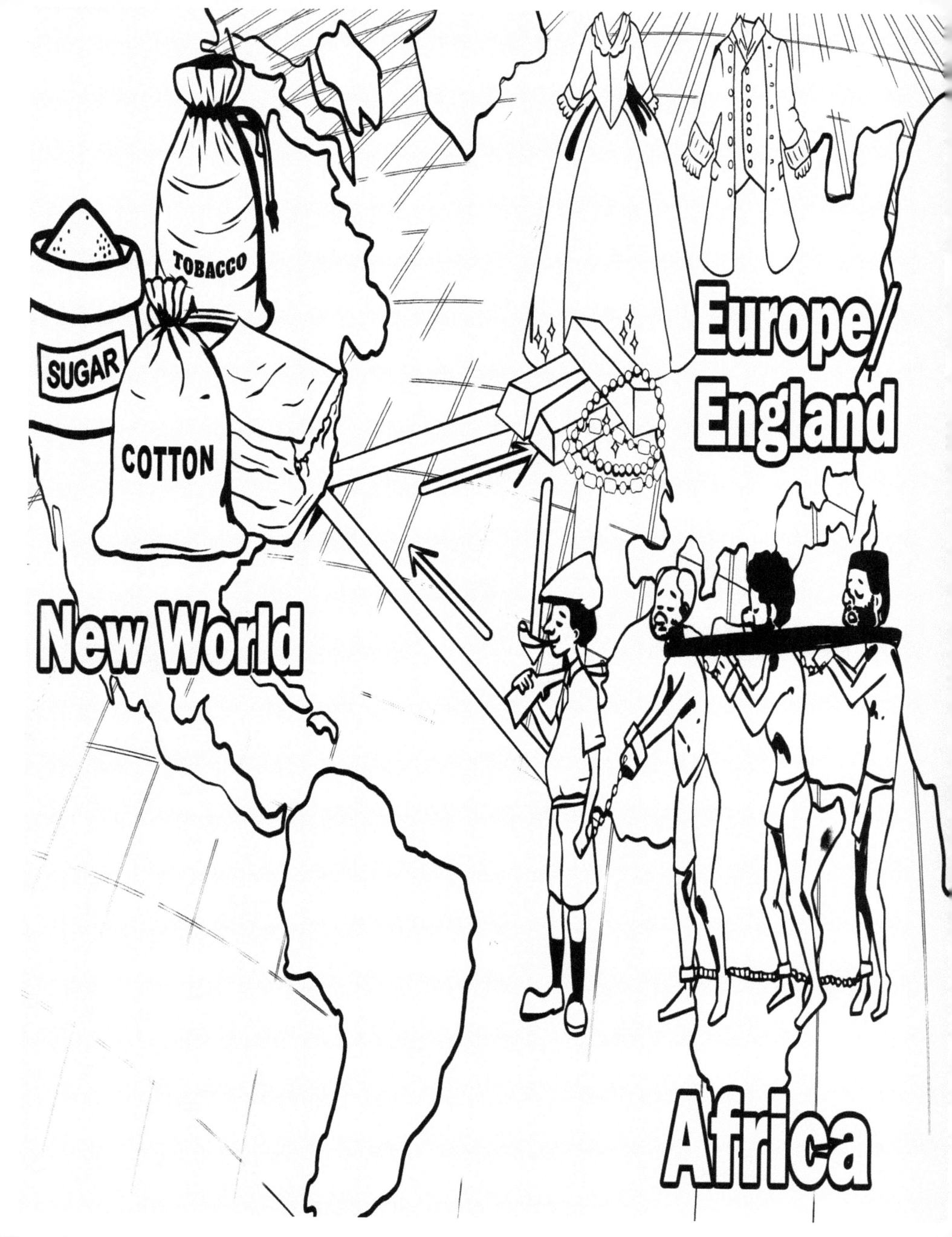

Juneteenth

Writing Prompt

Instructions: Write a detailed story about Juneteenth starting with the origin to present time. Use the coloring pages as a guide.

Answer Documents

Reading
Short Vowels
/ ă / cat, pass, yap, gad, at, alp, jam
/ ĕ / elf, leg, bed, sell, hen, bet, yell
/ ĭ / wig, hip, zit, rim, kid, gig, biz
/ ŏ / jot, mop, dot, hop, toss, mom, pod
/ ŭ / bus, bum, sub, nun, hut, cup, sum

Long Vowels
/ ā / said, table, bale, lake, tail
/ ē / meet, geese, deal, jeep, peep
/ ī / pie, pine, bike
/ ō / quote, zone, rote
/ ū / cute & mute

Short & Long Vowels
/ ă / apple, ram & sap
/ ĕ / net
/ ĭ / mint, clip, zip
/ ŏ / loft, cot, chop, pom
/ ŭ / mull, hum, nut, bun, hug, nun

/ ā / lame, tame, day
/ ē / keep, peak, feed, geese, me
/ ī / light, kind, lime
/ ō / nope, join, load
/ ū / mule

Blends
slap, treat, twist
grill, gulp, brain
guilt & milk
drum & spray
blend, crape, tomb
lamp & gold
left & trice

Diagraphs
perk, boil, hark, chime, thug
load, bird, phat, check
shaft, wreck, sung

shut, quiz, king, crash
graph
wind
wrench

Blends & Diagraphs
Blends-blind, clumsy
speak, slum, drip
malt
slide, trap, crime, plea, slot
treat

Diagraphs-dark, ore, sheep
path, form
check, shop
fork, lack, bird, sharp
that, meow, perch, out, might
Both Blend & Digraph
slur

Blends & Diagraphs
Blends-climb, dump, sleek
front, stomp, coil, sleet, bride
left, spice

Diagraphs-shark
panther, torch, thicker
chirp, math, painter
sharper
meow, perch, gout

Both Blend & Digraph
store, speaker, slumber, slacker, sprang,
snicker, story

Short Vowels
Answers will vary.

Long Vowels
Answers will vary.

Nouns and Verbs

Nouns and Verbs Activities	Objects List
1	astronaut aquarium award ask astrophysicist
2	bank island bridge boil bandage
3	daddy dance dig dinner drive
4	foot orange fountain lemon fishing
5	cubes/blocks iron leaves island record

6	key stove kite knife kayak
7	magazine book tissue napping notebook
8	question marks quail parrot tractor blanket

Sentence or Fragment #1
Sentence
Sentence
Fragment
Fragment
Fragment
Fragment
Fragment
Fragment
Sentence

Sentence or Fragment #2
Fragment
Sentence
Fragment
Fragment
Fragment
Sentence
Sentence
Fragment
Fragment

Sentence or Fragment #3
Fragment
Fragment
Sentence
Sentence

Fragment
Sentence
Fragment
Fragment

Sentences will vary.

Math
Matti…8 balls
Kate…6 cookies
Gabbi…3 pages
Kat…13 balls
Lexi…54 dolls
Pete…$4.07
Jay…16 pages
Cassidy…8 eggs

Science

Lava Lamp
Answers will vary.

Plants
Answers will vary.

Living and Non-living Things
Living Thing
Cow, octopus, butterfly, plant, child, fish, dog, pig, bear
Tree, meat (uncooked)

Non-living Things
water, boat, airplane, tire, book, money, television, mailbox
house, bed, meat (cooked)

Sink or Float
Sink: egg, pen, can, fork, key
Float: cotton balls, feather
Sink/Float: fruit will vary.

Social Studies

Community Helpers
Answers will vary.

-er	-or	-ist	-ian	other
teacher	doctor	cardiologist	technician	chef
singer	professor	cosmetologist	librarian	surgeon
barber		scientist		nurse
painter		biologist		president
banker		therapist		principal
designer		artist		detective
baker		meteorologist		
firefighter				
engineer				
cleaner				
cashier				
loan officer				
minister				
plumber				
waiter				

Family Celebration
Answers will vary.

Innovators
1st row: Benjamin Bannker (clock), Sarah Boone (ironing board), Marie Brown (home security system)
2nd row: Fredrick McKinley Jones (refrigeration system), Rebecca Crumpler (medical book to treat diseases in infant and young children and women in childbearing years), Garrett Morgan (traffic light and gas mask)
3rd row: Octavius Catto (baseball league and civil right activist)

Wall Street Activity
Answers will vary.

Black Trivia
1. C
2. B
3. C
4. B
5. C
6. B
7. B
8. A
9. C
10. A
11. C
12. D
13. B
14. A
15. A
16. B
17. C
18. D
19. D
20. B
Bonus: B

www.ingramcontent.com/pod-product-compliance
Lightning Source LLC
Chambersburg PA
CBHW041516120626
46551CB00018B/2449